Pat Winslow

Unpredictable Geometry

Templar Poetry

First Published 2008 by Templar Poetry
Templar Poetry is an imprint of Delamide & Bell

Fenelon House,
Kingsbridge Terrace
Dale Road, Matlock, Derbyshire
DE4 3NB

www.templarpoetry.co.uk

ISBN 978-1-906285-21-0

For permission to reprint or broadcast these poems write to
Templar Poetry

A CIP catalogue record for this book is available
from the British Library

Typeset by Pliny
Graphics by Paloma Violet
Printed and bound in Turkey

In memory of Julia Sunderlin

Acknowledgements

Brando's Hat

Carterton Pride – Tin Shacks to Beacon Town

Fin

Not for the Academy (Onlywomen Press)

Poems 27 Lancaster Litfest Anthology

Rain Dog

The Reader

Stand

Writers Inc

ARTS COUNCIL ENGLAND

Contents

Wild Horses

The horses were running again last night,
bellowing in the dusty bowl of earth.
The sweat was slick on their backs.

Above them, the Perseids flashed like zippers.
The world was spinning towards morning.

Now, their movements are laconic,
a flick of the tail, a toss of the head.

A blackbird chips the bone china air.
The day's like dazzling crockery,
stacked and ready to fall.

The Boot at Barnard's Gate

There was a time, a day like this, when
the tree was just planted and the late sun

buttered a tub of marigolds. There was a day
when all they heard were cows and the hay

being got in, the call of a distant great tit.
Each man wore a dark blue jacket.

Some had bicycle clips but most had tucked
their trousers in their socks. A day of heat

and ticking insects. They stretched their toes
inside their boots and leant their elbows

on the bar. Each man watched his beer
foam up inside the glass. Already, they were

dreaming it in their mouths, cool and bitter.
Autumn yeast, fallen fruit and fresh leaf litter.

No plane from Brize Norton, no trailing
screams, no slur of traffic, this maiming

swish, this hiss, this sound we often take
for silence. You could sing and crack a joke,

hear the matches scrape, smell the Woodbines,
ride home hands-free along the unlit lanes.

On a Train Going South

Three men walking down the slope of a vineyard
and a Kentish woman hanging out her washing
after a week of rain make you want to cry.

You have to look away, check you've got your ticket,
text a friend, eat a sandwich. You don't know why.

It's like those other times – a girl skipping, someone
with a bag of shopping, a man singing under a lamppost.

There's a boy who's been staring at his own reflection.
He's stopped. Now he's staring past his face at you.

He might be feeling the way you did one afternoon
when you watched your mother walk away from school.

How brave she looked. How home seemed a place
of endless little efforts. Distance only increases sadness.
Like seeing England from a plane or the world from outer space.

The Copse

There are signs and messages – two slender boles
crossed at the apex, keeled over trees, natural walls.

A rope ladder climbs an oak. There's a shelter of logs,
a loose interlocking of branches, some as thick as legs.

The smell is bluebell and fox. There's a pink flash,
a spill of thunder, a staircase of limestone and brash,

slabs carked out of the earth, hobbled through nettles.
Something very old lives here, something that settles

and comes to rest like a book that keeps opening
at the same page. Something quiet is happening.

You walk through, fumbling stones like rosary beads.
Everything is in its place. Untrammelled weeds,

spiders' webs like skeins of smoke. You feel like a ghost.
In the presence of God is not quite right, but it comes close.

Ghost

I read once of a shadow burned into the ground,
like an autumn leaf, a black imprint on a shiny street.

And there were patterns the silk kimonos left, wounds.
A girl and her mother had weeping flowers for scars.

Here, there are blokes in offices who control the locks.
There are panic buttons. Don't tell me the man in the cell

has seen it all before and isn't scared. Don't tell me he's hard.
It's not the dark he fears, who's died before. It's the years,

the interminable mopping, the young men shuffling
in slippers with plastic spoons in the dinner queues.

It's the absence of anything that's green or growing.
A single blade of grass might save you from madness.

How did it sound, that shoe lace, when the knot pulled tight?
Did the bars that took the strain creak before they settled down?

To find him like that, blood stopped up, lying in shit.
To cut him down like Christ and pick up the phone.

Each time you pass you see him standing there. You remember
how he'd turn and grin. Sometimes you imagine him being born.

The Coodham Papers

1. The Mother

I don't remember when he came,
when she started talking about him.

I used to stand behind her
and watch him take shape in the shadow
I was casting over her shoulder.

Whatever I said, she'd never look up.
In any case, I didn't want her to stop.

Was that his breath I heard, his
soapy skin I smelt? I began
searching for clues. He was

everywhere – on the floor, in her desk,
on tracing paper, in exercise books –

and nowhere. I tried phone directories,
ancestors, the deeds to the house, wanted ads.
I even looked amongst the obituaries.

Then came the fear of unlocked doors,
people I hadn't met yet, neighbours.

How could a child of four dream
such a man? How could she be so sure
of the way he spelt his name?

2. Coodham

Brown is my favourite colour.
Like her eyes. And mine.

One day when I'm
looking in the mirror

I'll see her again.
She'll walk with a stick

She'll have a sloping back
and papery skin.

Sometimes I hear a radio
and I start to fumble.

My fingers scrabble
like I'm washing a potato

or picking over fruit.
The smell of grass and clay

tells me she's close. One day,
when she's least expecting it,

I'll go through those doors.
I'll be inside her head.

We'll sit down and read
the news. She'll pause.

She'll marvel at my undeath,
the miracle of my return,

the disconcerting fact that I can
breathe through her mouth.

3. The Box Bedroom

Did he stoop, take her hand and shake it solemnly?
Did he tell her his name? She doesn't remember the day

or the way he stood or the smell of him. Just how
scrubbed he was, how like a windfall of apples he was.
His trimmed moustache was as neat as a mouse.

His hair was brown and smooth. He kept it short,
combed to one side. The parting was immaculate.

He'd be thick-necked and bald by now. Burly.
His white stubble might gleam in certain lights.
His shirt buttons might strain across his belly.

He could be sitting behind her even now, watching.
How young he was when her aunt killed him.

Twenty. No more than that. *He looks like Hitler.*
She looked up in disgust. When she turned back
there was a crayon drawing on a sheet of paper.

They were in the box bedroom. He was like snow.
He melted so quickly she never even saw him go.

The Dressmaker

Penury was surely that small room.
The smell of static, the crush and rustle
of satin, the crackling petticoats.

It's a wonder she didn't go mad.
It's a wonder she didn't go blind
sewing sequins all night.

Hours and hours counting
the halves and thirds, turning hems,
stitching velvet collars and piping,

her fingers scrambling like spiders
in the button tin, in the evenings jabbing
pins in the cushions on the mantelpiece.

Bolts of material on her shelves,
tissue paper in cardboard boxes,
yellow organdie scallops, flowers.

She had photos of famous people on the walls,
a tray of boiled sweets on the window sill.
She wore gold slippers and stretch trousers.

She was listening to the plastic radio
she kept plugged into the light socket.
There was something about an anniversary.

She kept her head down. She was frowning.
Young soldiers, flamethrowers, Belsen.
You could see the tattoo on her forearm.

The needle kept pricking in and out,
small popping noises, accurate and quick.
It was a thing of beauty. The tattoo.

That she'd survived, that she could do this.
She wore her sleeve rolled up.
The shame was theirs, not hers.

The Devil's Dog

I was glad to go. He never smiled.
He never said a friendly word.

A dog likes to be fondled sometimes,
sit side by side, companionable.

He was too obsessed with solitary matters,
the gathering of wood, washing, mending.

Look at him now, standing like a fencepost
at the corner of the field.

Look at the wind clapping the pages of his bible.
What does he see? What sanctuary does he find?

When he asked for the bridge I saw my chance.
I watched the builder set up camp.

I watched him hauling stones each day
and work them into wedges.

He laid them on the grass
and carved strange marks in them.

The heat from his body was intense.
I licked the salt off his hand.

I stood thigh-deep in the shallows
and buried my head in his crotch.

He gave me scraps
from the tip of his knife.

When the keystone was in place he called
my master – The first to cross, remember?

The builder caught a fish that night.
I saw it glinting as he pulled it in.

My master woke from his celibate sleep.
I crossed when he turned his back,

when he took out the book
and started mumbling.

All That Shiny Life Gone

A drake at the side of the road
and now this crow hanging
in a farmyard tree.

We can't bear brilliance.
We must have diesel
and barbed wire

and throw up lights
so we can monitor
our shadows.

We watch TV.
Each night's the same.
A million pixels a minute.

A man carries a child
in a repeating pieta
past a row of tanks.

We eat dinner.
The kids play outside.
The phone goes.

Emails and letters shock.
A newspaper headline.
Someone you knew.

You accept because you have to.
There's no other way.
Heartbeats that ran out.

Everything runs out
sooner or later.
Except bombs.

See how they catch the sun,
how phosphorous screams
through our skin.

Death is beautiful.
If we didn't love it
we wouldn't do it.

Daly's Scarecrows

All summer there were rags and twists of rope on his tiled floor.
His grainy hands heaved sacks of straw and coats and shirts.
He sewed on buttons and hunted out the missing pairs of gloves.

Hats made him cry. Sometimes he rolled a cigarette and stared
through the smoke, thinking of coins and polished shoes,
the truck journeys that rattled through the dust and mud.

Later, they stood on his hill, with names stitched onto their backs.
They had gifts in their pockets. Small things. A child's harmonica,
sixpence, chalk, an apple, cigarettes, his father's broken wristwatch.

Pyrrha and Deucalion

Sometimes I dream us back again.
He's staring at the leaking roof,
wondering when it's going to stop.
I'm bracing the door against the ooze.

The world's burst open like rotten fruit.
Bloated carcasses glide past our house.
One nudges the window. He's panicking.
What if there's only us?

Even today, the ground's not safe.
There are twenty stones I keep inside a jar.
He thinks I'm crazy. *That was then,* he says.
I'd like to hide them from him, but where?

Every morning I count them.
He says we're blessed. *Tomatoes,
radishes, olives, figs. Forget the past.*
I can't, I say. I know what I know.

Last night I dreamed a red cat,
a sandstone pebble that turned in the sun.
It licked the top off the milk. Miraculous,
the click of its throat, the flick of its tongue.

But those others. Heavy, stumbling, clack-limbed.
We didn't care at first. We tossed them as we ran.
We were sowing the earth that day.
We dug the stones out with our hands.

The mud released them slowly.
Each one came away with a gentle plock.
I threw first. Nothing happened. I threw another.
He climbed to higher ground and tried a rock.

This isn't working. No, I said. Listen. A spurtling.
See where we've been. Like fishes flailing. A roil
of hands was finning through the broth, finding light.
And behind us, suddenly, out of the heaving soil,

carved heads, a monstrous budding of shoulders,
torsos, hips and legs. A whole thicket of them
clambering forward, their great knees cracking.
Our progeny. Not God's. We gave them form,

determined what shape, colour, texture, size.
His spawned men, mine spawned women.
No child among them. I watched some rising
from a spew of anthracite. About a dozen.

A fiery race, industrious. He threw a lump of flint.
It cracked in two. Twins, smoke-blue skin.
One of them was frowning, chewing a nail.
His brother looked at me and grinned.

More! my husband shouted.
I watched him pick up a handful of shale.
He was leaping like a goat,
drunk with it all.

He scattered white men everywhere.
Brittle voices, angular bodies.

He tipped some gravel into my hands. I let it fall.
Sharp-nosed women with glittery eyes.

Stop, I told him.
He was rolling boulders down a hill.
A race of giants, monosyllabic,
piggy-eyed and brutal.

He was pitching stones all night.
By morning there were thousands
marching north and south, east and west.
The sea was giving us back the land.

Now he ploughs the fields
and tends the vines. He hoes and irrigates each line.
He's military. Precise. Food's become a science.
He inspects the fence and cleans the barn.

I don't walk barefoot any more.
How many lie suspended in the earth's dark yolk?
Each day I listen out for cracking twigs,
hands smashing through the undergrowth.

I sleep with one eye open.
Most mornings I wake up screaming.
Grey machines in rows behind our trees.
They're heading this way, silent, gleaming.

The earth opens up and folds them in.
A muscle cuts off their air supply.
I clutch his rigid back. He says nothing.
For weeks now, he's been watching the sky.

Layover

You're watching the Manhattan skyline
from the Brooklyn Bar at Newark airport.

Over there, where the sun is dipping, someone
is giving birth. It's certain a child is laughing,

that a boy has piano practise, that there are lovers
and dog walkers. Restaurant workers dice onions.

Grandmothers turn on TVs and take showers.
Fathers eat pizzas, hug their kids, read stories.

Cell phones ring, people turn off lights, a widow
makes a pass at her best friend. Your waiter

wipes the table and stares past you through the window.
A blue sky can lie. Like it did in Hiroshima or Basra.

A Salute

In the beginning

It's an enormous decision. The hand
that grasps mine so tightly takes me beyond
small-town Boots and Woolworths. Round the corner
and through the door leads me away from her.
She brings me to myself. I become shelf,
bracket and wall. I learn the art of stealth,
discover shadows, the cat's underworld
of tables and chairs –

Go and play outside!

I grow fat on torchlight feasts, an expert
on under-blanket research.

Go on out.

I don't notice her ribs or the sharp points
of her elbows, the swollen scrubbing joints
of knuckles.

Get some colour in those cheeks.

Sometimes I can be gone from her for weeks.

Unravelling

I love the easy creak of new wicker,
her fat basket on wheels. We bend over
to move oranges and spring greens aside,
to make room for six well chosen books, hard
books in greasy see-through plastic jackets.
Later, over tea and ginger biscuits,
I decode stains – the pustular remains
of a prized vesuvius, small hairlines
of blood, encrusted scabs, sly black footnotes
that pose as asterixes. So discreet,
those snot blobs at the bottoms of pages,
those tiny acts of boredom. Teenagers,
boys mostly, have a grooming ritual
when a plot gets mired in too much detail.
But acne and bogeys don't quite compete
with that other thing they do late at night.
All that furtive business with handkerchiefs
can fund the imagination for weeks.
How do they hide it from their Mums?

                                                            Patsy!

How?

      Put that book down now. Come and help me.

Now we are thirteen

One day I decide to move to Adults,
do the moonlight flit from flat to bedsit.
The rooms are strange, partitioned, L-shaped, eaved.
Others are airy, large penthouse suites carved
by the slow track of the sun; elegant.
Sometimes there are neat privets in the front,
roses, trees. I am more the blocked drains sort –
cabbagey sinks and sweaty football shorts,
Victory gin, cheap cigarettes, a cough
like cracking timber, lincrusta walls, moths,
mice, mould, God knows what. I have sex – bad sex –
and abortions in crumbling back to backs.
I even commit murder and incest.
I top myself in a lighthouse – swing east,
south-east, south, south-west – a clone on a rope.
When Jimmy's trumpet brays all the lost hope
in the world, I am barely eighteen,
but I know what I've seen in the cold sheen
of pock-marked kettles and leaking taps –
lives as normal as chipped and broken cups.
(Our crockery is under lock and key.
I haven't learnt to raid that yet. One day.)

The pay-off

What are you doing?
                    She grows suspicious.
She was bound to.
                    You're much too serious.
Look at your face. You frown all the time.

There's a V above your nose.
                    Thinking lines,
and a new threat – inky fingers.
                                        Willful.
Selfish. You're preoccupied.
                    Over hill, over dale,
thorough bush, thorough brier. Up and down
the people go. One afternoon, late June,
the steam hissed. No one left and no one came.
The heat.
                    You've gone away. You're not the same.
You've changed.
                    Unwontedly.
                                        Listen to me.
It'll come to grief.
                    Into the valley
of death rode the –
                    You're like a closed book.
Open it. Share it with me. Let me look.
What are you doing?
                    Storming Aqaba,
lying on bellies, no food, no water.
I'm murdering kings and washing my hands.
I'm trying on crowns and measuring lands.
Hollow Harold has lost his eye and I

am wading through miry bogs, blade held high.
Wet leather is thonging my wrists and shins.
My skin is hairy and coarse. I'm a man
astride a horse. My cohorts are weary.
See how the tide plucks and knocks. See how we
must live behind bookshelves. Twenty-three months
hiding from windows – so many of us! –
all pale as mushrooms in the Prinsengracht.
And the sword blade dives into Becket's back,
poor Catherine's hand catches the glass, Magwitch
asks for files and wittles, two sticks are clutched
between gown and flesh, a soldier's rough cross,
the fire is lit. She calls Rouen, Jesus,
her boy's head turns, her body burns, her heart
is cut out and thrown in the Seine, intact.
Enough!

There's more. Listen. Slow black crow black –
Enough!

Moles creep –

Enough!

It's a ship-wreck

ship-shape night –

I said –

There's never enough.

Oh, what a face, what blue-grey eyes, what loss,
what fear, what never-had-in-the-first-place.
She gives me the key and in the short time
between unlocking and finding, I'm
grappling hooks, rope and kit bag. I'm a thief,
an acrobat, a steal-by-night. No leaf

unturned. I am not hers. I am my own.
Separate. It is a big decision
to take your daughter's hand and lead her out,
to watch her go through your personal gates
of terror. She sees me eat privilege
as though it were simple bread, draw knowledge
like well water. There is a border post,
she says, and the sentries are childhood ghosts.
She cannot or will not cross. To this day
we wave from either side and walk away.

New York, 1961

Everything was black and upright in those days —
bicycles, typewriters, cars. Our phone was a miracle,
a solid bakelite thing that sat on the window sill
with its silver exchange button glinting in the rays

of pokey sunlight. At Christmas, we'd get our call
from America. Armoured cables under the Atlantic,
her voice torpedoing through the planktony murk,
so close she could be standing next to us all.

'What's the weather like?' we'd say, too stunned
by the length and the depth to think of anything else.
'Snow.' Copper threads, coaxial, like TV aerials,
vacuum-tube repeaters, a ship with a rotating drum,

spooling and spooling like the longest crap in history.
'They're skating in Central Park.' Her voice smiles
and cracks at the same time. 'How are you?' The miles
are grey and sad like I know my aunt's eyes must be,

like my mother's are when I pass her the receiver
and go and stand in the garden with my sister.

The Balloon

He keeps hold of the balloon like it's the last note
of a favourite song. He's watching the years rotate
like wheat fields. How long now since he listened
to the hiss of snow or watched an ant crawl around
a crack wide enough to take the edge of a man's hand?

He's so tired these days, he's so quiet and well kept
and precise in his sharp number one prison haircut.
This balloon. He tells me about it again and again.
How it travelled past his window one afternoon,
how he watched it turn into a dot on the horizon,

like an event that might never have happened.

The Bride

The groom and best man
parade her through the dust and litter.

She drags a train
like synthetic cream behind her.

Sometimes she stops
and they bend to tidy it.

Twice round the park,
past a boy with a football,

past a girl reciting
the breathless monologue of her life.

The bride looks over
and the monologue girl falls silent.

Empty bottles roll in the wind.
She glides off over leaves and guano.

The monologue girl starts up again.
Her bloke scratches his smelly dog.

There's a pause. They're watching us.
Two middle-aged women

with shoulders touching,
eating ice cream.

The Chewing Factory

Slab-heads, great hoofy chunk beasts
hefty-heaving through iron gates to the field.

Their mouths set to work immediately.
A fugue that sometimes synchronises like clocks.

Again and again, their muscular tongues
renew the gleam of their nostrils.

Their bodies are huge maps rippling in the sun,
continents and islands straddling white sea.

Hay barn stomachs dance the grass about.
Cuds emerge like tight wads of Kleenex.

All day they stand, their gable ends to the wind,
eyeing the world and magnifying it.

It's a miracle how hay gets to be so fat,
how sap ends up creamy suds in my blue jug.

The Season

You're lying in a strange bed, watching
yellow headlights range across the walls
and over the ceiling. Each slow hush
is like a mantra, how a curtain falls

between acts and rises again. The house
has a way of breathing. Its evenings are calm.
Here, you roll on your stomach in the bath.
This is what it's like to be able to swim

with bubbles crackling around your ears,
footsteps and voices through the overflow,
seagulls and dogs, the sound of the world,
and your mother's plates clattering below.

Except they're not her plates and the rhythm
is nothing like home. There's time to listen
in the morning, to weigh a book in your hands
and turn the pages before making a decision.

Romany customs and folklore, the heart
of England in a horse drawn caravan.
Books no one would think to buy you.
Books you'll probably never see again.

When it comes to packing and waiting
for the taxi, you have a head full of birds
and rivers, secret codes, wounded pilots,
spiders, pirates, bilge keels and lee-boards.

You feel as though you've crossed a red line
on a map. The train to London is smaller
than you remembered. Your flat is shabby
and cluttered and the girl up the road is taller.

When you see your friends, there's a chasm
your words keep falling into. How strange it is
to feel this new, how your skin keeps touching
your school uniform in all the wrong places.

Cutty

The florin and sixpence in the purse
is her mother's trust in her.

She'll hop skip and jump down the road
look left, look right, look left again

and cross and cross the great big ocean
the wide Sargasso of cars and buses

all on her own to the Express Dairy
which is blue and white as the foaming sea.

Yo ho ho for a packet of tea and a bag of sugar
some milk and some butter to melt by the fire

when the sad coal scuttles and shunts
like worn out tired old siding engines.

See how the apricot sun is descending
how the cutty surf threads between green, gold and red

and she doesn't stop she runs instead
to the razorbill sharp bird-flapping edge.

She has ruby earrings and a black-tarred pigtail.
The snakes on her arms, which the first mate drew

with some ink and a nail whilst the crew wasn't looking
she swapped for a kiss when the lookout slept.

Her cutlass is lean as a scolding tongue.
Her limbs are as strong as any boy's.

She climbs up the rigging and scratches the sky
with her sailor's grin and her chart-maker's eye.

See how the petrels are towing her out
past pebbled seals and switch-backed dolphins.

The cormorants dry their boomerang wings
and plunder the peaks for silvery fish.

Her lungs are rasped by the captain's smoke box.
Oh how the petrels are towing her out.

Lagoon! Lagoon! The gold doubloons of inlet sound.
She climbs down aft and rows her shallop out.

She shanties the buck and ridge and swell
and drags her boat to the scrunty rocks.

She ties it up with a mooring hitch
and watches the skin of the ripening sun.

Her galleon rides the crease and furrow
safe as a baby, safe as a baby.

It's rocked from its belly by the anchor below.
The wood, the masts, the ropes turn black.

She watches, she waits and now, at last,
the sun begins to swallow the sea,

drinking it from the tilting cup
on the other side of the world.

Too soon! Too soon!
The first mate rings the angelus bell.

Her kissing mate rings the ship's church bell,
St. Edward's Catholic Confessor bell.

He calls her back to the dry bone land
and dusty, dusty evensong.

Heave-ho to the red bus Finchley Road,
Hoop Lane and all the traffic lights

to the semi-detached October evening
with her mother's order under her arm.

She's walking home to the fire and the sink
to the liver brown lino and the things that click

like dentures, knitting and electric lights
with tuppence ha'penny in the purse, her mother's trust in her.

Under the pillow where her dreams spill out
is a bloody nail and a bottle of ink.

She's planning things, great future things
in the blotting paper silence.

Nobody sees the dragon rise,
my sister's earth-spinning dragon rise.

Nobody sees its east-west eyes.
Nobody looks that far.

Didcot Parkway, Monday Morning

The man putting caution signs on the wet platform
has an aura like an electrical stutter. There's no asylum
from his past, no way to switch it off. The visual hum
surrounds him. He has no choice. It's 10:31 precisely.
He's watching the soldiers taking his parents away.

In the forecourt, a woman clutches a bag. Her coat
is buttoned up to her chin. Her wet shoes are tight.
She's lost on the beach. Her knuckles are white.
Her blue light stammers. It's important to choose
a meeting place. Let them come and find you.

Now the shivering slipstream of a businessman
puzzling the ticket machine, the gold octogenarian
fumbling for a coin, silver inspectors, neon signalmen,
the twilit Philippino who makes coffee. Her memory –
Mama's pesos in a jar, nappies, the smell of poverty.

And his – how flames eat wool. His – standing on one leg,
spelling the entire Liverpool team backwards so his dog
won't die. So many. One roly-polys to a first snog,
one eats snow, another ice-skates to a Beatles' song.
The procession of lights goes on and on.

In the Caffir Cardi Café

The women have pencilled in eyebrows.
They sit with navy handbags on their knees
and shovel chips and peas onto steel forks.

They dab the corners of their mouths
at frequent intervals and chew silently.
Their elbows are always off the tables.

When they finish, they leave their cutlery
in the middle of their plates. One sips tea.
They nod to one another and start to talk.

They take it in turns. The first to speak
crosses huge varicose legs. Soon, they're all
shuffling around and fiddling with scarves,

making their own news, drawing their own
conclusions, dispensing advice like pills.
Then one by one, they get up, pay and walk out

into the pre-wrapped vacuum-packed century
where God is a camera and you can watch people
sleeping, buttering toast, dancing and crying.

1954

England was gravy, stew, brick alleyways,
dark shoes, hats and gloves, coal scuttles.
Post Offices and railway stations were thick
with tobacco. Pennies clattered in toilet locks
and till trays. You could smell the crackle
of a thousand Bakelite radios warming up.
Every grin said Bisto, Oxo, Marmite, HP.
Every raincoat was bacon and strong tea.
A grocer in a tan cloth coat emptied potatoes
into paper bags, women wore scarves knotted
under their chins. Chiffon was a word you'd
never forget. Landfill was a word you didn't
know yet. There were adverts on TV. Persil
washed whitest. The telephone rang sometimes.
The Ascot banged and rattled in the kitchen.
Colour was sudden and brilliant. Fruit Gums,
lipstick, a city bus looming through fog and
at 8:30 in the morning, your blood on the sheets
as the exquisite roar of milk filled your breasts.

The Call

When you wake, it's to a missed heartbeat.
There's no fumbling. Somehow your feet
know where to go. Someone has your number.
If you get this, call Auntie. I need you to call her.

The lights. Bedroom, landing, stairs, office.
You're in your skin, playing it back. *Auntie.* This
is going to be bad. The worst bad imaginable.
You've got your address book on the table.

If you don't call her, it's like Schrödinger's cat.
Life can go on. You can stop it. Except that
you've started tapping the codes for the country,
and each number makes it more real, more likely.

Her voice is thin and rasping. She can hardly get air.
Are you ready for this? It's your sister Julia. Julia.
You don't believe in Schrödinger's cat. You're sitting
inside your skin, cold, cold, and you're hitting

the numbers, imagining desert dust, police lights and now
your mother in her nightie, whose feet know where to go,
who's picking up the phone, who's just got out of bed,
who knows before you tell her that her daughter is dead.

Flight

Hauling out into the sky above Tucson,
the first thing I do is close my eyes and lock
onto a grid of streets in a fold-out map
and zero in on dust and thumping tyres,

the leash, the key, the bottle of water,
the cell phone that went missing,
the hair tie, the sneaker which came loose
and a utility pole that still looks the same.

The man who saw it happen, mentioned your wrist –
he didn't say which – and I thought of you
holding toast, your hands on the keyboard.
How many words a minute? I never did ask.

A faint pulse. You were hardly there and yet
on some deeper level he thought you might be.
You might know that someone was working,
keeping you alive till the paramedics came.

Not to have to live, that's the best I could wish.
The research hospital where you'd worked
couldn't even use your skin. Your boss
did the brave thing, opened the door, walked in,

saved us from doing it. *Yes, this is her.* Is, not was.
Hauling out into the sky, I have a neat plan
of minutes. You're tying laces, picking up the key,
clipping on the leash and checking your phone.

I can't prevent this. You're already turning
the corner, walking over stones, pulling
your hair tie tight. The morning smells clean.
Your dog sniffs a bush. You look west

then north – some bird perhaps –
not hearing it come. Your bones snap.
You're flying thirty foot in the air.
You hit the pole and stop.

You're unbroken and beautiful and lying
on the ground – this bit isn't true – lying
like you're on a lounger, enjoying the sun.
You're thinking of sex or slipping into the pool.

How it used to be. A book beside you. A towel.
Not how you were when the police came
and sprayed paint around your legs and head.
Not how you were when your boss saw you.

Blunt traumas. Contusions. Multiple fractures.
I take a grid, this plan, this familiar place,
this truth and untruth which I hug close to me,
all the way to England and my mother's face.

Autopsy

Less than 24 hours after, you're wheeled out
in a plastic pouch. You're undressed except
for a sock and sneaker on the left foot.

In the pouch are a cut away dark blue sports bra,
a sock and a cut away pair of black short pants.
They don't say what happened to the other sneaker.

I can spread my hand behind and above my left ear.
We were the same hat size. So, here's where you gaped,
here's the fractured skull. And here, and here.

The hair is blond, straight and about 6 inches.
They don't mention the humid days, how it used to
go into kinks when I rolled the window down, which

annoyed you, though you never said, or how I'd find
strands of it long after your plane had left, how I liked
to hold them up and turn them in the sunlight on my hand.

The 2nd through 7th ribs bilaterally show fractures.
There are also fractures of the pubic symphysis
and left wing of the ilium. Someone must have pictures

of you dancing. I still have that video we made.
Partial separation of the right sacroiliac joint is noticed.
Before the Gulf War. 1991. All summer-long we partied.

There are fractures of the proximal right tibia and fibula.
The distal left forearm is fractured. And now I remember
all those minor breaks you had when we were at school.

In and out of hospital, me phoning up, taking you home.
Big sister, little sister. Not any more. The body is that of
a well developed, well nourished, middle-aged white woman.

It's 63 inches and weighs 117 pounds. There are tattoos.
The pubic hair's been shaved. Copper-coloured nail polish
is present on the fingernails. The irides are blue.

I can go further than blue. They were dazzling and heroic,
trusting. The news report, of course, is show-biz –
that photo your neighbour took last month is iconic.

The posterior body surfaces show no significant scars
and the anus is unremarkable. Now I miss your humour,
your email sign-offs. Sister Mary Fibrocystic Hyperplasia,

Sister Mary Circle of Willis. Your brain comes in at
a round figure of 1,350 grams, which says nothing
of what you were thinking when the vehicle hit.

You heart weighs in at 270 grams, which says nothing
about the weight of grief or the width of my loss or the depth
or the height or the shape of anything any more.

Five Things I Have Cause to Remember

1.

Last night we were on the bus to school.
Your hands were holding the metal rail.

I waited for your bottom lip to drop
when the bus pulled out from the stop.

Every morning, all the way there,
straight-backed and silent, that stare.

What was it you saw when you wriggled
out of your uniform, when you struggled

to get free of the white shirt each morning?
Was it just her warmth you were wanting?

2.

The day you went missing, not understanding then
what sisterless meant, I saw myself call your name.

I was on TV. My face was the moon.
My legs, as I ran down the road, were not my own.

I went from bush to bush, the likely places,
not thinking of the obvious answer which was

a lift home with a friend and, finding us not in –
we were at the school – turning back again.

Seeing you drive through the gate undid the rope,
the knife, the police car, the man in the coat,

the posters and the headline news, the front-page
photo of you smiling, fixed forever at that age.

3.

That time you dropped a rock
on my foot

and our mother laughed in shock
or when

you punched my arm the day I came back
from hospital

and burst the stitches where they took
the cyst out,

not to mention the time you rode your bike
into me,

still doesn't make up for the fact
I tried to kill you.

4.

The mist came and I was almost sisterless again
in the white, in the endless, in the quiet roar of panic
which rushed the ears.

The hiss of the sea, the steamy calm that morning,
the east and west and south and north, the nothing
ness of it all.

The beach stones cracked and rolled. Our mother's
voice loomed through the fog. You clung to her.
I was adrift

and loving it, the delicious fear
of finally being
alone.

5.

I tried to find the scar where your mudguard tore
into my ankle. I thought I still had it but over
the years it must have disappeared.

I'd like to tattoo it back into my skin.
I'd quite like to feel it hurt again.

I want that spar and clash, that flash of anger,
the feeling that your bones and mine were
unbreakable as long as we had each other.

The Piggy Back

Finally, I mourn. You're on my shoulders.
We're rattling over tarmac. The handlebars
judder up my arms. A long swoop to the sea.
Platinum waves, dogs, a buff coloured bay
that curves for miles. It's right the older one
of us should survive to do this, that you lean
over me. You've earned the vantage point.
Here's to every death defying fast descent
I'll ever make. Here's to a week of solitude
that's been the opposite of grief. The flood
of self-pity never came. There is no tidal bore
of sorrow. It's not as if you haven't left before.
I should have known it wouldn't be dramatic.
I should have expected this vast grey Atlantic.

The St Dunstan's Man

You know the world again,
but differently.

Smell has a colour
and touch has a shape
more honest than
you can imagine.

When he holds an egg in his hand
he learns how the world breathes.

He can build a chessboard in his head
and plan your next move.

Today the sun
beats like a heart.
On days like this
he see boys drowning

in clean hospital beds and remembers the weight
of guns and medals in equal proportion.

Between the lavender and honesty
is the last person he saw.

He walks like rain
on new hoed earth.
Weightless gravity
is how he survives.

This is what it's like. Radishes,
onions, tomatoes, kale, potatoes.

He measures each day
and lives.

White Van Woman

See her against the drum-roll sky.
A box on the horizon knocking
curves out of hills.

She has an oblong view of the day,
wing mirror eyes.
Her shoulders are like ham hocks.

She's used to wardrobes and bookcases.
She calculates the exact degree
in an angle of manoeuvre.

The engine shudders.
Her palm is on the gearshift,
throwing first then second.

Cruising down the East Lancs,
she goes fourth and fifth,
glides like a swan to the lights.

Down the A39
past Mr Meat and Two Veg
slapped up against the tank of his Harley,

past Lada Man
with his windshield knocked out
and bits of polythene flapping.

Rock FM in her cab
over Wenlock Edge
with a four poster in the back.

Under archways of rainbows
to the Exeter turn off.
A fridge and sixty pairs of jeans.

She drinks coffee from a flask,
finds a Polo Mint in her pocket
in the thick of a tailback south of Macclesfield.

Listening to Meatloaf
over the thrump of tyres on cats eyes,
she thinks how a fork lift chunks into place,

how a Luton might look below her window.
She imagines a job where the cheque
is there at the end of every week.

An Encounter, Breach Wood Fair

Diving's like descending a ladder of light
into the jewelled silt of the night.

Green ideas roll at you. A fart
might be a silver pebble in a dry suit.

At sixty feet you can lose a sense of place.
East and west don't seem to exist,

therefore time and war don't exist.
It's just you, two lungs, a belt of weights.

Once you came upon a sunlit anchor
in the cold press of English waters.

There were red anemones on a conning tower,
a chain encrusted with Dead Man's Fingers.

I can't stop watching the way your throat
rises from your woodman's shirt

and marvelling at the forest of white
hair on your chest. I wonder what

it must be like to be you at eighty,
tanned and wiry, a vigorous certainty

about everything you do? The ability
to shape and turn ideas, the muscularity

of your storytelling doesn't lessen.
I'm still in the grip of your imagination.

Joe's Lantern

It swings – dangerous wasp-light –
black to yellow, edge of cheek bone
to the edge of chin and back again.
Sometimes it fills his night with terror.

His eye sockets dance. Swivel ho!
The prow-end ups and heels. The ship's
caulking expands beneath the ropes.
The seesaw wind grinds in his ears.

He never imagined this, lying on his
Essex hill, sap-stained and happy,
a rime of sweat under each arm,
picking his teeth with grass.

Two weeks later, below decks,
his skin's already glow-worm white.
He's forgotten what fixed earth feels like.
Soon, the clasp of ice will tempt him out.

Blown glass spinning in the sun,
a sheath that's grown overnight
on rail and mast and chain.
In his diary, in his neat hand, he'll write

Icebergs are the cathedrals of the sea.
He'll have forgotten this lurching dungeon.
He'll hesitate on some sidewalk where the snow
rises like boulders against the kerbstones.

He'll dodge a horse, pat a dog. Downstairs,
in some bar, a nickel will rattle on a counter.
When he takes the mug of frothing ale,
he'll look up and see the lantern there.

And the journey will begin again.
Seven wagons. New canvas stretched
taut over hooped wood. Twelve men,
one woman, swaying towards the sun.

A stranger's map. Going west.
This heat. This dust. Burrs in his shirt,
a hole in his boot. He'll build a fire,
brew coffee, listen to the coyote's drawl.

The light will still be there,
yellow and constant as the moon
that followed him. It'll fill his mouth.
Even as he takes his last breath.

The Kid

Her skin was too white. She was hot and piggy
in her bundle of clothes. The way she walked
towards him, the luggage, the label they'd put
around her neck. He could tell from her eyes
that fear was a sort of adventure. He'd never
beat it out of her. She'd study him like some
arcane language, make secret lists about him.
She'd wear the loss of her mother like an amulet.
Soon, there'd be a new coat, pyjamas, jeans.
She'd smell like family. The school bus would
pick her up. There'd be books and toys, friends,
a metal typewriter. And no word from England.

Densitometry

The machine's unzipping your scars,
unpacking your skin. Up and down
it clicks and hums, until you're
without ligature, without elasticity.

You're reconstituted colour by colour.
There's a web of bone on the screen,
dense, like the entrance to a nest.

A spider could sit in there. Or a bullet.
Something fat, pulsing like poison.

When it's finished, your scatter-graph,
is close enough to either side of normal
to be normal. But it's the bike ride home
that makes you feel less vulnerable.

It's the stretch and pull, the ability to
think sideways and swerve and bend
that gives your body weight and mass.

Up and down you go, hard on the pedals,
breathing in lead, particulates and CO_2.

Burly

The big man rows out to a place
where we can hardly see him.

Frail as a leaf now, he assumes
the position of a horizon.

He causes us to look often.
We cannot resist turning our heads.

See where the wake widens out to touch us,
where our footprints subside.

His eyes were like warm metal.
He was the ballast.

So many footprints now.
The winter sun is on our backs.

A cold wind has been blowing for weeks.
How we've stooped.

How we've bent to the contours of loss.
It astonishes us how easily

we make room for it, how willingly
we adjust. Like a womb or a cave.

It fits perfectly inside the rib cage.
How strong and burly grief is.

It's a Lovely Day Tomorrow

She leans against the wall like a foldaway chair.
She's so clackety she can't reach things any more.

In the afternoons she drinks the sun like milk.
She drinks it deep. Her dreams are petals falling.

Some nights she creeps around – things
she's forgotten or remembered.

You'll find her staring by thimble light,
her hand resting on a remnant of material.

Or she'll be emptying a drawer of photos,
letters, string and sealing wax.

There's a song she keeps singing.
If she had a piano she'd play it.

There are Kilner jars on the floor,
apples, pears, damson jam.

Her clock is set for six.
It's the best time, she says.

Up and about before the rest of us.
Leading the way.

Handbag Stories

1. Twisted Sister

Molly's, which was navy blue,
opened and shut like an argument.
You couldn't get a comb in edgeways.

Lucky if you found the lipstick,
or the hanky scented with Devon violets
she used to dab her nose with.

It was full of tests and riddles –
guess which mood I'm in today,
guess which way the wind blows.

Snap snap – the huge jaws on her lap,
her buniony hands crossed on top.
She'd sit for hours, biding her time.

2. Iron

God knows what the baroness kept in hers.
I have a theory it was empty.

The real business was up her sleeves,
ice blue, thin as razors.

Even now I dream of her
switching the lights off one by one.

3. Roger

The bin liner followed him like a dog.
One kick was all it took.

Crumpled clothes and leaking biros,
enough unread papers to start a fire,

a notepad and a stack of batteries,
a Walkman, Playboy, unpaid bills,

3 lbs of potatoes, Marmite, beans,
Blue Stratos deodorant, condoms, tea,

the 18th Brumaire of Louis Bonaparte,
Hegel, Marx, the Saturday Pink,

scattered everywhere like rumours.

4. A Perfect Marriage

Dot and Roy didn't have children.
They had a tartan bag on wheels
that she would push and he would pull.

They filled it with bottles.
Empty on the way down the hill,
full coming back.

They did it twice a week,
three times if it was Christmas.
No one ever heard them row.

5. The Niece

Mine was Tibetan, stripes and bells, carefree,
worn on the shoulder, swinging with books
from Golders Green to Finchley Central.

Who could have guessed the miles
from Lhasa to be here?
Who could know the frozen roads?

They slept behind rocks, rode trucks,
turned up in dusty refugee camps.
They missed the smell of butter.

My aunt brought back some chhurpi.
I chewed it for weeks whilst composing
letters to children in Dharamsala.

Tashe Delek means good luck.
A swastika symbolises endless time
and protects against evil.

Writing was an act of faith
I kept long after the bag
grew threadbare and fell apart.

Gowpen

In the absence of a bowl, two hands
scooping water after a long journey,

a cascade of diamonds, skin splashed
clean of dust, slaked thirst.

It could be the beginning of a fire –
dried moss, birch bark trimmings,

a match on a stone, a whisper
of smoke, cupped and blown.

It could be an offering – petals thrown
on a bride, flowers picked for a dead child.

Or something small. A butterfly
or bird set free from a room.

It could be an allowance of grain,
one person's entitlement for a week.

It could be as simple as please.

De Hoog's Gift

De Hoog's fingers work quickly.
Finches are his speciality.

He breaks their necks first
and threads their heads into
a split stick he carries.

He rings each group of ten
and sells them door to door.

There's a widow who keeps
the bones for toothpicks.
He likes it when she smiles.

He brings her gifts from Delft.
Her children never go without.

Sometimes she visits the druips
and spends all day with him.
The youngest wants a linnet.

He'll take a needle and hold it
over a steady candle flame,

one thumb stroking the throat,
a forefinger cradling the head
whilst he sears the eyelids shut.

Blinded birds sing more sweetly.
Gisela won't know it happened.

Stroke

All it takes is nineteen muscles.
First comes a pencil and four lumbricals,

getting her hand in the right position.
She knows it so well, it's like a reflex action.

She remembers a desk, carving her name on it.
Trying to hide it. A slap when the teacher found out.

There was an inkwell she used to fill each Monday.
A pen for getting into Med School. Seven interossei

and now various flexors, extensors, rotators.
A pile of books on a table, elaborate pictures.

She remembers spilling coffee once, the shock
of his cool hand on the back of her neck,

the way he slid it inside her bra. Flexor carpi radialis.
The muscle bends and turns the hand at the wrist.

Their graduation, the way their gowns flapped
in the wind. Blossom. Then confetti, nappies,

first steps, first shoes, working in the early hours,
clamping and stitching, knotting, cutting. Extensors –

indicis, digitorum and pollicis. Chart notes
for a team of unseen transcriptionists.

Writing articles. All it takes. Nineteen muscles.
A well sharpened pencil and four lumbricals.

If she could just find the word for the area.
Broca's. The picture is so clear.

Salt

The moon pulls and pummels the earth.
Every day the tonnes are washed up
and dried in pans on the water's edge,
stowed in sacks and bags, transported
on the backs of lorries, shovelled into
bins and metal containers and hoisted
into the holds of ships and iron tankers
for the bag filling factories of Kent,
the depots of Leeds and Birmingham,
the shops in Bolton and Huddersfield,
small concerns that sell methi leaves,
haldi, coffee and pickled cucumbers.
A little kindness in salt, a little bitterness
on the tongue, on the rim of a glass
of margarita in a bar in Manchester,
in a single tear that waits to be cried.

Fit-up

It's like
the dark insides
of a humming box.

Night's lit
by profiles and spots.
Day is Light Straw and Nile Blue.

Time passes when
a woman stops talking
and it goes to black.

You might never see her again.
Fade up. Q birdsong.
There's a book about us.

Irena (that's me) X down stage right,
light candle, move centre left.
Sometimes I think my thoughts

are pre-ordained,
that I've said these words
again and again.

I have a theory
that God is a technician.
At his right hand sits a sound engineer.

I have no proof, but here
it rains a lot and nothing gets wet.
There are owls and no one sees them.

No river, either.
Our path stops dead.
The acacia has no roots.

We're being watched.
I hear coughing sometimes.
I don't sleep well.

Time's running out for us.
A man with a clipboard says.
We're counting the days,

watching the lights
come on, go off.
Time passes.

The Golden Boy

He died when the England flags were out
and motorists were lethal with testosterone
and booze. Our water butts were empty.
It hadn't rained for months whilst he'd been
hollowing himself out. He was a bed of bones.
His long finger kept pointing the way.
It's easy to go if dying's what you do best.
A little bit less each day. Sometimes hunger
can fill you up. It's all you need. But his eyes
had the whole sky in them. It was hard to
believe he'd really do it. All that laughter.
Mountains make a fine farewell if you're inclined
to see them and snow and ice can be as crisp
as sheets. Think of arms and legs and the length
of a spine. There was strength in his fragility,
an alpine perfection in his final breath I hope,
repose in the summer heat. The lights keep
changing. Leaves are crinkling on the trees.
Nearby, a boy is bouncing a ball and chanting
England. The air still smells of possibility.

Slope

Sliddery with a wine bottle
to the end of the garden in big stubborn boots.

It's a rammel down there, loppings and branches,
a scramble tangle of clippings and dabby compost.

Her cigarette makes a pirling spire to the sky,
a soft curlicue thinning out to nothing.

In her throat is a spawl of spit.
She gobs it onto the darkening blades of grass.

Blue evening closes in across the canal.
Mist invents itself out of the afternoon.

On the ground, by her feet, boring insects
operate beyond hearing.

A frass of defecated wood
rises like a city of tea leaves.

There's a smell of mint in the shadows.
Swallows are arrowblading.

There's a glim of sun in the wake
of a passing moorhen.

She's untying the knots of a recent argument,
splicing the silences together.

Each sip of wine brings a new resentment
bursting like blood in her mouth.

Portrait, Thirty-Seven Years On

Her small hands are sinewy and clever
on the key board. She's focused, doesn't blink
or swallow. The afternoon sun makes her frown.
A sudden shock of rooks causes her to look up.

She remembers her father's face at times like this,
imagines what his inside-looking-out felt like.
The corkscrewed smile, his eyebrows. He's there
looking at her from the wedding photo on the sill

with her mother – that other self she feels most
when she's telling a story or laughing, when
she's animated, showing her teeth. Something
hamstery about her then. Something soft and fat.

A wobbly chin. And now she's licking her lip,
feeling it prickle and sting with summer sweat,
Marmite, the wind across the field at the back.
She looks closer, stares. And feels scared?

She hasn't looked this closely since she was 17.
A stranger then. And here she is again at 54.
All that life, all that's happened in between,
breathing, looking back at her and measuring.

There's something falling in and pinched now.
Something skewed or leaning. The lopsided
jowliness of her, the fuzz on her cheeks, silvery,
despite her young girl's hair, which is her father's.

Since this is a portrait she must have objects
which tell us more. Piles of books coated
in fine dust, CDs and pens, a diary that won't close,
a mobile and a land line, a poem on her screen.

And things that acknowledge death. An old cat
sleeping on her desk, a skeleton, a medical prank
dressed in suit and tie. And something to show wealth
Or lack of it. A VISA bill. And finally, her partner,

walking in behind her, late from work, bearing flowers,
who sees the scene she's looking at, who sees
the back of her head, the things she cannot see, the stoop,
the golden frame of sunlight, the shape she'll leave behind.

How Ice Is Formed

Thin wands is how it starts – or seems to with the naked eye –
and some are peacock quills. Others spread like leaves
flattened and beaten under the hammers of the moon.

On colder nights they hinge into a featherscape,
an interlocking of wings, like a swan's been trapped
beneath the surface, its last gasp hidden by a dead white span.

Worse is the frozen silence, the ring of iron
when you skim a stone to the other side, the traffic cones,
a Coke can on the injured back, the battlefield of sticks.

By day it creaks and shifts. You dare not walk on it for fear
of drowning. You stand and stare and think of open mouths,
bubbles held in suspended animation, bullet-time photography,

the strength it takes to unbend a pond and lock another year
                                                    in place.

The Trapeze Act, Carterton Day Centre

Forty feet above us, measuring the spaces,
the angles of return, the give and take of rope and wood.

If you were counting heartbeats it was only
so you wouldn't miss and fall.

Nipp and Rollo, stars in intricate constellations,
going from darkness into light.

It takes practise. It's just a job.
Your hand keeps flying from table to chair.

Everyone's watching. You've made us all
part of your balancing act and it's breathtaking

how a memory can leap from person to person,
how you have us all swimming through air.